Complete Sentences

A **complete sentence** tells:
- who or what the sentence is about
- the action that is taking place

I am sitting on a tack.

Look at the groups of words below.
Put a circle around the complete sentences.
Cross out the groups of words that are only parts of sentences.

1. on the soccer field

2. marcus went into the store

3. my best friend

4. do you want a slice of pepperoni pizza

5. let's paint our bikes a new color

6. in my backpack

7. the rock group was playing loud music

8. i flew in a jet plane to my grandfather's for summer vacation

Sentences

There are four kinds of sentences:

Statements tell or state something:
Toni went to the park after school.

Questions ask something:
Did Toni go to the park after school yesterday?

Command sentences command or make a request:
Don't go to the park today. Be careful.

Exclamations show strong emotion:
Going to the park after school is a great idea!

On the line after each sentence, write the kind of sentence it is. Put the correct punctuation at the end of each sentence.

. - statement and command
? - question
! - exclamation

1. Is the cheetah the fastest land animal _____

2. We enjoyed our trip to the olympics _____

3. Begin your science projects this week _____

4. Don't go so close to that steep cliff _____

5. Have you studied about dinosaurs in school _____

6. Where do gray whales go in the winter _____

Write Sentences

| statement | command |
| question | exclamation |

Make two different kinds of sentences using the words in each box:

| the red fox |

1. _____

2. _____

| hurricane |

1. _____

2. _____

| the soccer game |

1. _____

2. _____

Changing Sentences

Change these statements and commands into questions:

1. Many mollusks live in tidepools.

   _____

2. Jerome's science project was about plants and soil.

   _____

   _____

3. Wear your raincoat today.

   _____

Change these questions into commands or exclamations:

1. Can you help me?

   _____

2. Did you save your money?

   _____

3. Will you bring me the stapler and the scissors?

   _____

   _____

Run-on Sentences

A **run-on sentence** is two sentences together without end punctuation to separate them.

run-on   They were well-prepared they won the battle.

correct   They were well-prepared. They won the battle.

Read the sentences out loud to hear where one sentence ends and a new one begins. Put in **capital letters** and **punctuation marks.**

1. we like hot weather we always go to the beach

2. the bean seed sprouted it grew three inches

3. the Nile River is very long it is located in Africa

4. it is fun to do a science project just find an interesting topic

5. she read an amazing story it told about the old west

EMC 4030

Mouse Escape!

Read the run-on sentences on pages 6 and 7 out loud to hear where one sentence ends and a new one begins.

Put in capital letters and punctuation marks.

1. Can you come over? I need help.

2. my pet mice escaped can you help me catch them

3. where do you think they went did they get outside

4. look out one just ran under your feet

5. did it go under that chair let's move it and see

6. i got him where is the cage

7. how many mice do you have we've found two

8. i have three mice one is still missing

9. there it goes it's under that shelf

9. can you open the door i caught the last one

10. that is all lock the cage carefully

11. would you like to feed them they like sunflower seeds

12. thank you for helping you're a good friend

The Strange Planet

Read the story out loud to hear where one sentence ends and a new one begins. Place **punctuation marks** and **capital letters** in this story.

what a strange place this is it doesn't look anything like Earth why is the sky so dark and the ground so bumpy

what's that i saw a furry shape dart behind the rocks over there it's moving closer help i can't get away my feet are caught in some weird sticky ooze can anyone hear me

wow what a scary dream that was i'm glad to be awake that's the last time I have a peanut butter and pickle sandwich before I go to bed

Subject and Predicate

Every sentence has two main parts:
   The **subject** tells who or what the sentence is about.
   The **predicate** tells what the subject does.

   subject
   <u>**Snow White and the seven dwarves**</u> ate dinner together.

   predicate
   The seven dwarves <u>**ate all of the delicious dinner**</u>.

Draw one line under the **subject**.
Draw two lines under the **predicate**.

1. The tiny insects scurried quickly from place to place.

2. Matt liked the peace and calm of the forest.

3. The pioneers in their covered wagons faced many dangers.

4. The natives of the tiny village celebrated with a great feast.

5. The dense, tropical rain forests of Brazil are disappearing.

6. The children in the class screamed for the winning team.

Write a sentence of your own. Underline its subject and predicate.

_____

_____

EMC 4030

Writing Sentences

Combine **subjects** and **predicates** from the boxes to make **sentences**.

Subjects	Predicates
the small insects	ate and slept outside
all the boys and girls	need sunshine and water
the immigrants	worked hard
how many animals	were in the park
plants	had traveled far
a group of gorillas	lived in the jungle
the men and women	laughed at the funny song

1. _____

2. _____

3. _____

4. _____

5. _____

6. _____

Singular and Plural Subjects

Most verbs use different forms with singular and plural subjects.

Singular subject - The girl **sings** beautifully.
Plural subject - The girls **sing** beautifully.

Circle the correct form of the verb to agree with the subject.

1. Mr. Tyson (*read, reads*) us a story every Friday after lunch.

2. They (*watch, watches*) the play quietly.

3. Pinwheels (*spin, spins*) around when the wind blows.

4. Pioneer stories (*is, are*) interesting and inspiring.

5. The students (*prepare, prepares*) for the assembly at 2:00.

Write sentences using these subjects.

| **wild animals** | **the explorer** |

1. _____

   _____

2. _____

   _____

Commas

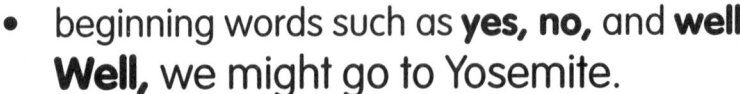

Use **commas** to separate:
- items in a series
  We ate **apples, dates, and nuts.**

- beginning words such as **yes, no,** and **well**
  Well, we might go to Yosemite.

- the person being addressed
  Susan, please bring me that tray.

Add **commas** where they are needed in the following sentences:

1. No they have not finished their homework yet.

2. We need to buy shirts pants socks and shoes for school.

3. Well you certainly did a good job on your science project.

4. Remember to bring your raincoat umbrella and hat.

5. Sam were you scared during that horror movie?

Write two sentences of your own that use **commas**.

1. _____

2. _____

Titles

Different kinds of titles need different kinds of punctuation.

- Titles of books, magazines, and newspapers are **underlined:**

    <u>**Charlotte's Web**</u>   <u>**Popular Mechanics**</u>

- Chapters of books, stories, television shows, plays, movies, poems, reports, and articles need **quotation marks:**

    "Popeye's Revenge"   "The Four Little Foxes"

- All titles need to be **capitalized.**

Read the sentences. Find the title used in each sentence and add capitals, underline , or use quotation marks where they are needed.

1. Our teacher reads one chapter of the long journey every day.

2. My favorite poem is stuart's worst nightmare.

3. Every Saturday morning my little sister watches the cartoon, the road runner.

4. We read articles from newsweek, time, and the daily herald to get information for our report.

5. I saw a movie called the return of the dinosaurs.

"When Someone Speaks"

- Use quotation marks and a comma whenever you are repeating someone's exact words.

  Mrs. Torres said, "Please close the door."

- Notice that a comma separates the words being spoken from the rest of the sentence.

Add quotation marks to these sentences.

1. I'm tired of carrying this bag of grain, said the hen.

2. The dog said, I won't carry it for you.

3. Then I will eat all the bread myself, replied the hen.

4. The hen complained, It is hard grinding the grain into bread.

5. The pig grunted, Don't ask me to help!

6. Well, don't ask me for any of the bread when it's done, squawked the hen.

7. The other animals complained, The hen is selfish to eat all the bread herself.

8. The hen thought, If they had helped, I would be glad to share my bread.

Colons and Periods

A **colon** is used when writing the salutation of a business letter and to separate the hour from minutes when writing the time.

Dear Dr. Smith: **5:25 P.M.**

Add **colons** where they are needed in this letter.

Dear Professor Patterson

Thank you for your help on my project. I will meet you at your office at 6 00.

Sincerely,
Jason Johnson

Use a **period** at the end of every abbreviation.

Prof. Salinas   **Mr. Edwards**

Add periods after the abbreviations in these sentences.

1. Rev Madison asked Ms Swanson to help him lead the singing.
2. Mr and Mrs Jamison left their keys in Ms Smith's car.
3. The students in Mr Jackson's class submitted their project to Prof Lowell to be judged.
4. The technician, Ms Rawlings, fixed our computer on Friday.

Apostrophe

Use an **apostrophe** to show possession:

- When the noun is **singular**, add an apostrophe and an s.

    a girl**'s** dress   the dog**'s** bone

- When the noun is **plural and ends in an s**, put the apostrophe after the s.

    two boy**s'** kites   the team**s'** caps

- When the noun is **plural and does not end in an s**, add an apostrophe and an s.

    women**'s** cars   the children**'s** coats

Add **apostrophes** where they are needed in these sentences.

1. The suns rays shone on the lakes surface.

2. The childrens rainboots were stored in the teachers closet.

3. The books pages were torn by the girls little sister.

4. The dogs tails wagged happily as Father gave them Johns leftover dinner.

5. We put Tonys books on the librarians desk.

6. Three girls bikes were left out in the rain.

Proper Nouns

All **nouns** name people, places, and things.
A **proper noun** names a particular person,
place, or thing and begins with a capital letter.

Margaret visited **N**ew **Y**ork **C**ity on the **F**ourth of **J**uly

Read these sentences.
Replace the underlined part with **proper nouns**.
Don't forget to begin each proper noun with a capital letter.

1. The children traded baseball cards and talked about the players.

   _____

2. The family went hiking in a national park on their vacation.

   _____

3. The teacher put a game on the table for free time.

   _____

4. The immigrants crossed the ocean and finally reached a new land.

   _____   _____

Nouns

Use the clues on page 19 to help you solve this crossword puzzle. All of the answers will be nouns.

Word Box

bees	sheep	teeth	Colorado River
men	children	moose	Tennessee
feet	geese	oxen	Lake Superior
women	parties	Saturn	bushes

EMC 4030

Nouns

Use these clues to help you solve the crossword puzzle on page 18.

Across

3. All the _____ wore colorful ties to the party.
5. How many _____ have you lost?
6. The _____ grazed in the field.
10. The _____ runs through the Grand Canyon.
12. _____ are taller than grass but shorter than trees.
13. _____ fly south for the winter.
14. _____ is one of the planets in our solar system.
15. _____ are larger than deer and have flat antlers.

Down

1. _____ is the only state in the United States with 2 n's, 2 s's and 4 e's.
2. My _____ hurt after standing in line for an hour.
4. The _____ begged the teacher to tell them a story.
7. Our class had three birthday _____ last month.
8. All the _____ wore flowered dresses for the party.
9. _____ is one of the Great Lakes.
11. The _____ were held together by a wooden yoke.
12. Many _____ flew among the flowers gathering pollen.

Plural Nouns

Most **plural nouns** end in <u>s</u>, but some nouns form their plurals differently.

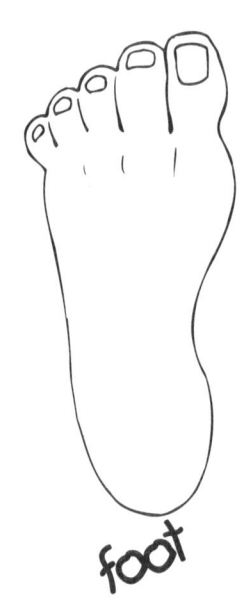

One	More than One
child	children
woman	women
man	men
foot	feet
ox	oxen
tooth	teeth
mouse	mice
goose	geese
moose	moose
fish	fish
deer	deer

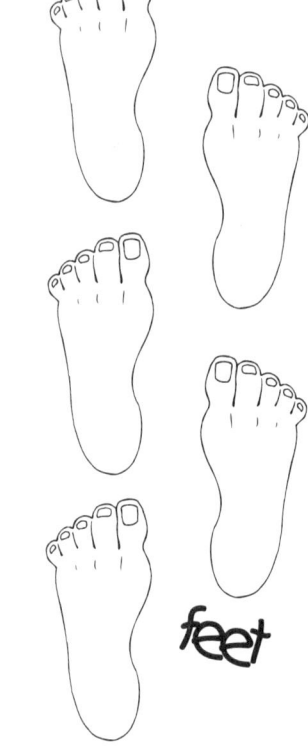

Change each singular noun in the sentences below to its plural form.

1. All the (man) _____ and (woman) _____ at the meeting agreed with the motion.

2. The cats on the farm love to eat (mouse) _____ and (fish) _____.

3. Before the storm, the farmers herded all the (goose) _____ and (ox) _____ into the barn.

4. At bedtime, the children washed their (foot) _____ and brushed their (tooth) _____.

5. The children often saw groups of (moose) _____ and (deer) _____ in the forest.

Pronouns

Pronouns take the place of a noun. They are used:
1. in the place of the subject
   I you she he it we they
2. to show ownership
   my mine your yours his hers our ours their theirs
3. to receive the action of the verb or preposition
   me you her him us them

Underline the **pronouns** in the sentences below.

Pronouns in the subject:

1. Joey and I went to the mall.
2. We bought ice-cream cones.
3. Joey and I asked for a new kitten.

Pronouns used to receive action:

1. Mom took Suzanne and me to the mall.
2. She bought us ice-cream cones.
3. Mom gave me a bandage for my hand.

Pronouns used to show ownership:

1. The students performed their play at 2 o'clock.
2. The dog wagged its tail when the girls came home.
3. We spent our summer vacation at Yosemite Park.

Using Pronouns

Replace the underlined nouns with the correct **pronouns**:

_____ 1. The class heard a good story today.

_____ 2. Steve and I want to go to the park," Sarah said.

_____ 3. "Tim got a shot from the doctor," Tim said.

_____ 4. The Moore family sent their friends postcards.

_____ 5. "Please give Joe and Tom a glass of milk," said Tom.

_____ 6. "Please take Steve and me to the park," said Sarah.

_____ 7. "It hurt when the doctor gave Tim a shot," thought Tim.

_____ 8. Their family sent the Moore family a postcard.

_____ 9. Jane's homework is in the drawer.

_____ 10. The family's car had a flat tire.

_____ 11. The horse's stall was empty.

_____ 12. The boy's shirt was hanging on the line.

Adjectives

Adjectives are words that describe a noun or pronoun telling what kind, how many, or which one

green	**enormous**	**Italian**
eleven	**none**	**terrified**

Underline the **adjectives** in the sentences below. The number after the sentence tells how many adjectives you should find.

1. We wandered along the crowded wharf to watch the tall ships sail into the peaceful harbor. **(3)**

2. The weary pilgrims trudged through the driving rain. **(2)**

3. Holding the multi-colored flag high over the heads of the triumphant troops, the brave captain moved through the cheering crowd. **(4)**

4. The talented actress gladly accepted the challenging role in the new play. **(3)**

5. The victorious team raced off the muddy playing field. **(2)**

6. Throughout the long, stormy night, the excited campers shared ghost stories and old legends of mysterious events occuring in the ancient valley. **(7)**

Using Adjectives

green slimy bumpy

Add adjectives to these sentences:

1. The _____ girls laughed at the antics of the _____ clown.

2. When the _____ teacher announced the names of the winners the _____ class cheered.

3. We wondered why the _____ man shook his _____ fists at us.

4. The _____ waves crashed against the _____ shore as the _____ birds scurried by.

Adverbs

An **adverb** describes the action of the verb, telling **how**, **when**, or **where** the action happened. Many times adverbs end with **y** or **ly**.

y or ly

Draw a circle around the adverbs in these sentences. Some sentences will have more than one.

1. The sun shone brightly on the blue water of the lake.

2. We walked quickly as the rain fell softly around us.

3. The teacher read us three funny stories today.

4. The Johnson family left for a camping trip yesterday.

Write sentences using three of these adverbs:

quietly   too   often
very   honestly   never

1. _____

2. _____

3. _____

EMC 4030

Describe the Action

Remember, an **adverb** describes the action of the verb.
Complete these sentences by filling in an adverb to describe the action.

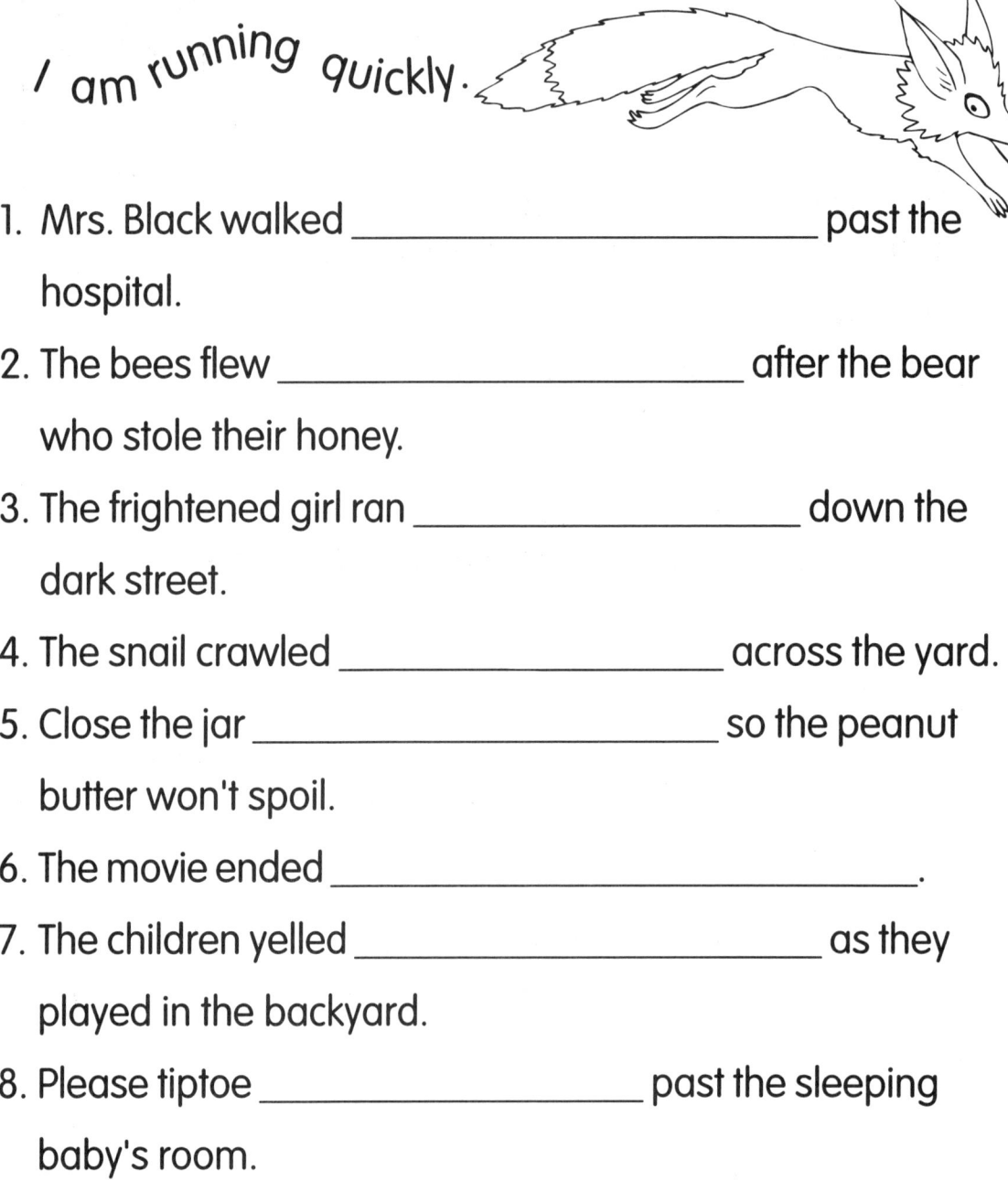

I am running quickly.

1. Mrs. Black walked _____ past the hospital.

2. The bees flew _____ after the bear who stole their honey.

3. The frightened girl ran _____ down the dark street.

4. The snail crawled _____ across the yard.

5. Close the jar _____ so the peanut butter won't spoil.

6. The movie ended _____.

7. The children yelled _____ as they played in the backyard.

8. Please tiptoe _____ past the sleeping baby's room.

Here are some words you might use:

angrily	quietly	carefully
sadly	happily	silently
loudly	slowly	quickly
tightly	blindly	suddenly

Verbs

Verbs are words that show action or a state of being.

dance think was feel

The correct use of some verbs can be confusing, especially these three verb pairs:

1. **may** and **can**
   May is used for **permission.**
   Can is used for **ability**.

   *You **may** not bring your football to the party.*
   *You **can** carry all three packages by yourself.*

2. **sit** and **set**
   Sit is used for putting a body in a sitting position.
   Set is used for placing something in another location.

   *The teachers told us to **sit** down and be quiet.*
   *Please **set** the dishes on the table.*

3. **lie** and **lay**
   Lie means to recline.
   Lay means to place.

   *I saw the cat **lie** down on her pillow.*
   *I **lay** the book on the table.*

Using the Correct Verb

Use the information on page 27 to help you write the correct word in each blank below:

1. **May** or **Can**

   _____ I stay overnight at Aunt Mary's tonight?

2. **lie** or **lay**

   The tired old dog wants to _____ down by the fire.

3. **sit** or **set**

   Please _____ that vase down very carefully.

4. **Lie** or **Lay**

   _____ the new clothes out on the bed.

5. **can** or **may**

   You _____ walk farther than you think.

6. **sit** or **set**

   Did you _____ next to Mrs. Gomez?

Irregular Verbs

Many verbs change from present to past in a regular manner by just adding **ed**.

Present:	Past:	Present:	Past:
play	played	pick	picked
walk	walked	dance	danced
want	wanted	look	looked

There are many verbs that do not follow this pattern. We call these verbs **irregular**. Some of these are shown here:

Present:	Past:	Present:	Past:
begin	began	go	went
grow	grew	know	knew
run	ran	see	saw
sing	sang	take	took
throw	threw	write	wrote
break	broke	choose	chose
come	came	drink	drank
eat	ate	fall	fell
spend	spent	freeze	froze
swing	swung	make	made

Use these irregular verbs to fill in the blanks in the sentences on page 30.

Using Irregular Verbs

Use the words on page 29 to help you write the correct verb form in each blank below.
Put a **P** over the verb if it happened in the past.
Put a **PR** over the verb if it happens in the present.

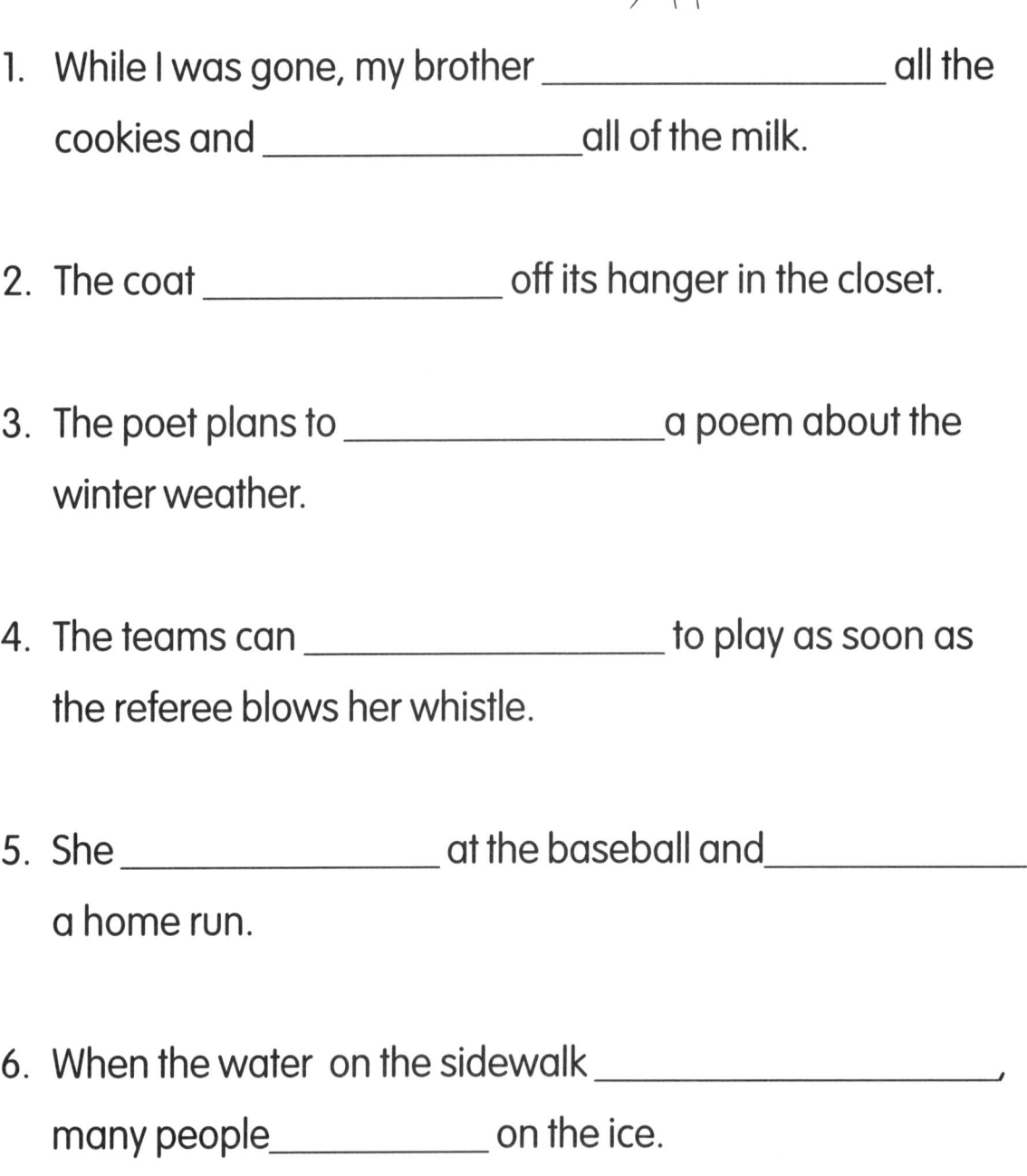

         P
He <u>broke</u> the window.
          PR
Let's <u>choose</u> a game to play.

1. While I was gone, my brother _____ all the cookies and _____ all of the milk.

2. The coat _____ off its hanger in the closet.

3. The poet plans to _____ a poem about the winter weather.

4. The teams can _____ to play as soon as the referee blows her whistle.

5. She _____ at the baseball and_____ a home run.

6. When the water on the sidewalk _____, many people_____ on the ice.

Answer Key

Please take time to go over the work your child has completed. Ask your child to explain what he/she has done. Praise both success and effort. If mistakes have been made, explain what the answer should have been and how to find it. Let your child know that mistakes are a part of learning. The time you spend with your child helps let him/her know you feel learning is important.

page 1

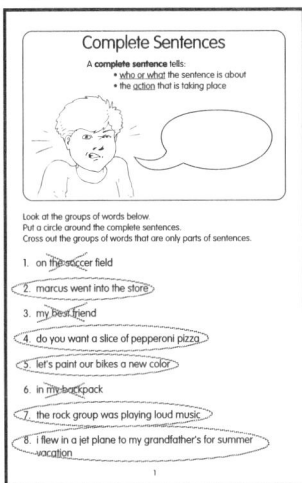

page 2

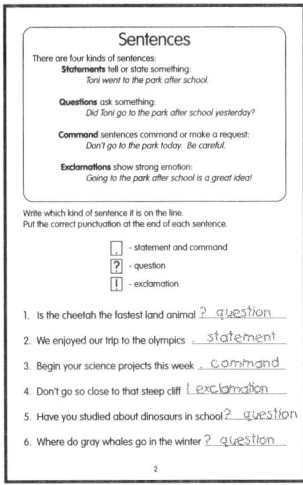

page 3

page 4

page 5

page 6

page 7

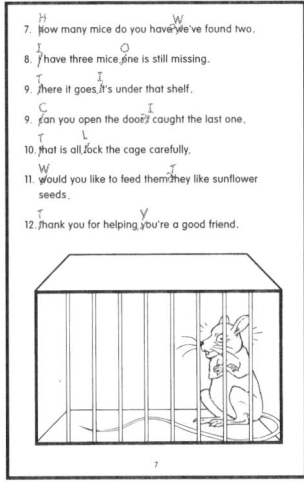

page 8

page 9

page 10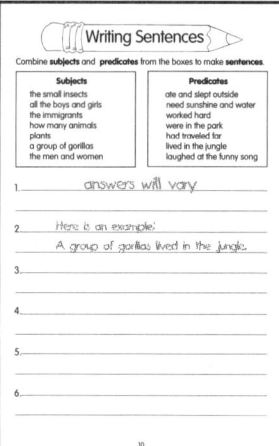

page 11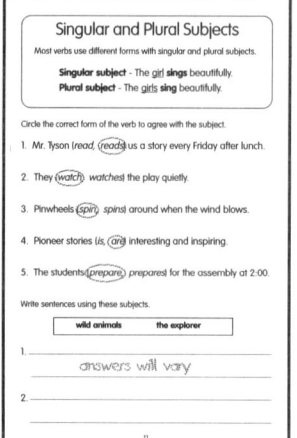

page 12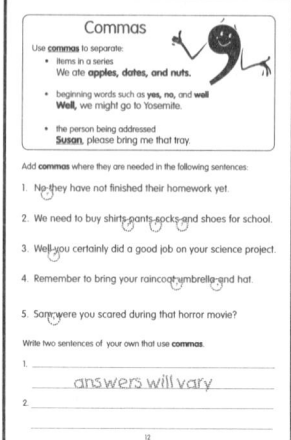

page 13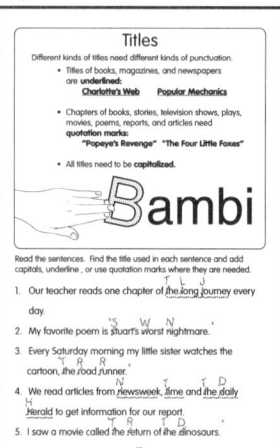

page 14

page 15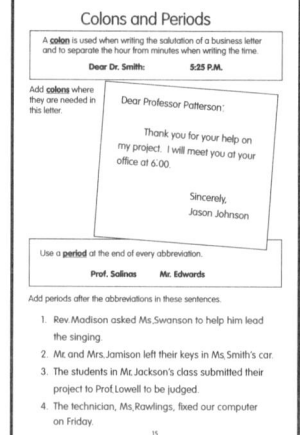

page 16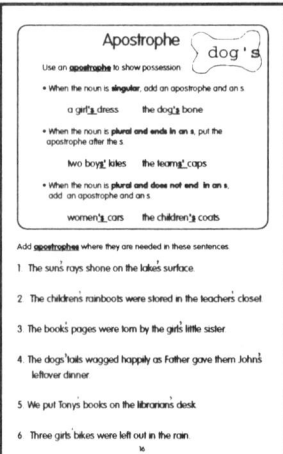

page 17

page 18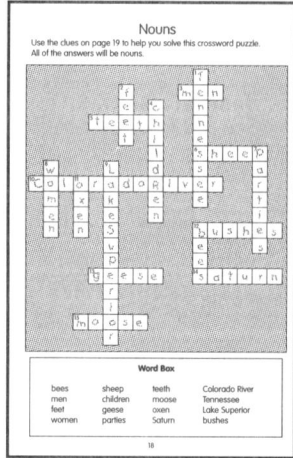

page 19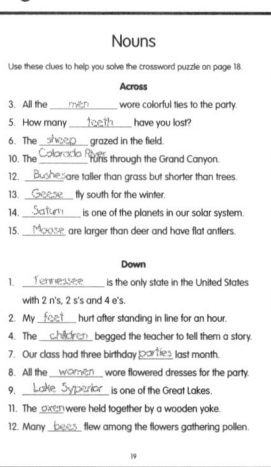

page 20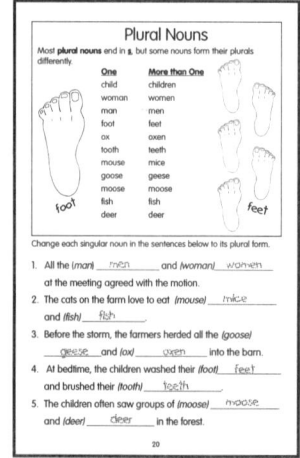

page 21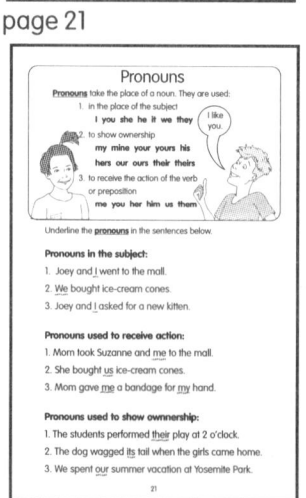